VIEWPOINT SCHOOL

Given to the Library by

Jillian Bleiweiss
for the wonderful year of
learning provided by Mrs.
Hurwitz.

June 1995

A Child's First Library of Learning

Amazing Facts

TIME-LIFE BOOKS • ALEXANDRIA, VIRGINIA

031.02
A

Contents

❓ Why Do Clock Hands Turn Right?

ANSWER The first clocks used the sun and shadows to tell time. They were called sundials. To make a sundial, people placed a tall stone in the ground. As the sun traveled across the sky, the shadow of the stone moved too. The shadow always went to the right. Years later, people made clocks with moving parts. They made the hands go to the right, just like the sundial's shadow.

■ A sundial's shadow

The sundial is a clock based on the movement of the shadow made by an object when the sun hits it. In northern countries like the United States, the shadows always fall to the north of the object and move to the right.

North

West

South

Do Any Shadows Go Left?

In countries far to the south, like Australia, the shadows from the sun fall to the south of objects. As the sun moves across the sky, the shadows always move to the left. If clocks had been invented there, the hands would probably turn left instead of right.

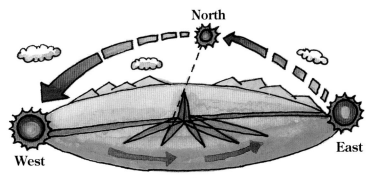

North

West

South

East

East

▲ **An ancient sundial in Egypt**

❓ Why Does a Week Have 7 Days?

ANSWER A day is the time from one sunrise to the next. A month is about the time that passes from one full moon to the next. Long ago people used these amounts of time to organize their lives. But they needed something longer than a day and shorter than a month. So in the ancient city of Babylon, 7 days were put together to make one week.

▶ **Market day in Babylon**

■ The Babylonian week

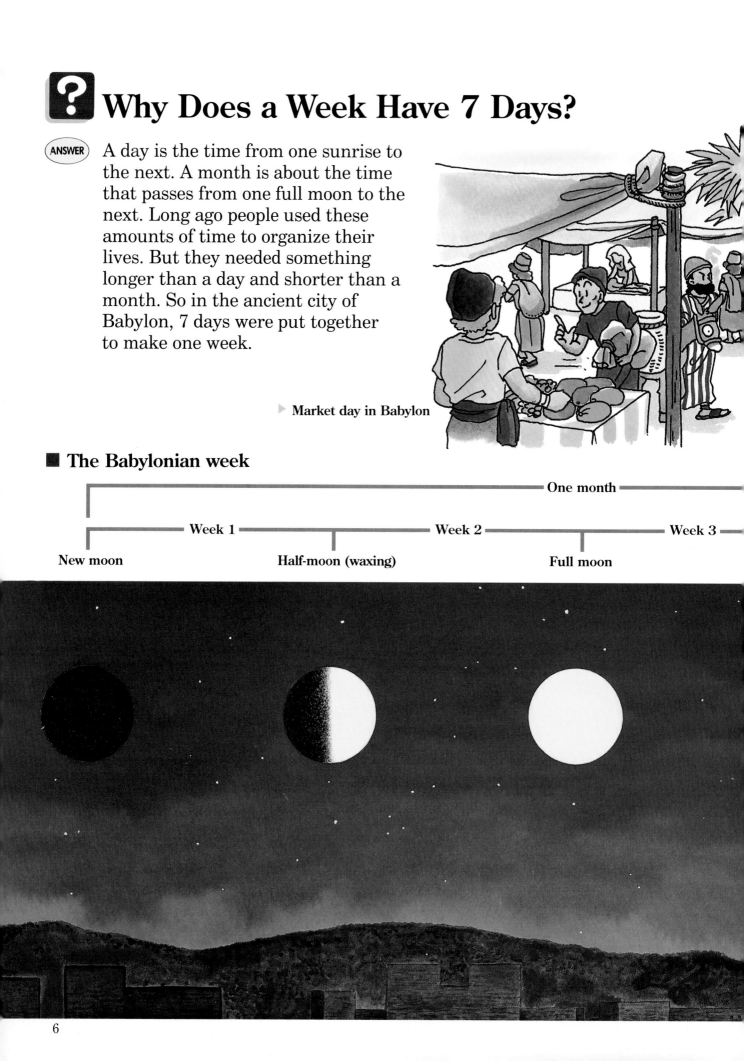

One month

Week 1 — Week 2 — Week 3

New moon   Half-moon (waxing)   Full moon

▲ A Greek week had 10 days

▲ A Roman week had 8 days

Week 4

Half-moon (waning)   New moon

The ancient Babylonians studied the phases of the moon. They used what they learned to make their calendar. The Babylonians saw that 7 days passed during each phase of the moon: new moon to half-moon, half-moon to full moon, full moon to half-moon, and half-moon to new moon. So they decided to make one week 7 days long.

Why Does Glass Break So Easily?

ANSWER When you drop a metal can, it may get a dent, but it does not break. When you drop a glass bottle, it shatters into many pieces. All objects—including cans and bottles—are made of tiny particles. They are much too small for us to see. The particles cling to one another. In some objects like metal they hold together firmly. In glass there are places where the particles do not hold together as well. That's why glass breaks easily.

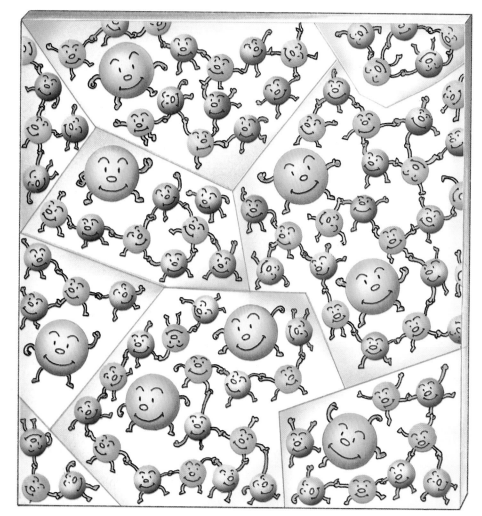

■ Structure of glass

There are places in glass where tiny particles are not "holding hands." You can see them in this picture. Those are the places where glass breaks easily.

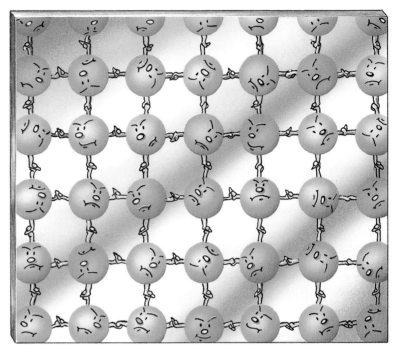

■ Structure of metal

Aluminum is a kind of metal. In this picture you can see how its particles hold together tightly. That's why aluminum is stronger than glass.

 ## Can Glass Be Stronger?

There are ways to make glass stronger so it is hard to break. One way is to put a piece of clear plastic between two layers of glass. Another way is to heat the glass in a special way so that it will be extra strong.

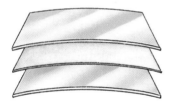

▲ Strong glass

▶ This is specially made safety glass. When it breaks, it cracks but does not fall to pieces.

◀ Heated-tempered glass is stronger than plain glass. When it shatters, it makes small pieces that are not as sharp as regular glass.

● To the Parent

The primary material in plate or bottle glass is silicon dioxide, the main ingredient in sand. When making glass, limestone and soda ash are added to the silicon dioxide. The raw materials are melted in a furnace and then quickly cooled. At this point, the mixture becomes molten glass that can be rolled into thin sheets to form plate glass or formed into other shapes. Sometimes special processes are applied during production to make glass stronger so it does not break easily. These methods include heat tempering, which is done to glassware that is used in cooking, or sandwiching plastic between sheets of glass, which produces laminated safety glass such as that used in the windshields of airplanes.

? How High Will a Balloon Rise?

ANSWER How high a balloon climbs depends on the kind of balloon. A small helium balloon that you get at a party will go up about 6 miles. A giant balloon that can carry a person may rise 20 miles or even more. Scientists also send up balloons with instruments that study the earth. These balloons often travel up about 25 miles.

▲ The arrows in this drawing show how wind moves around the earth. Sometimes balloons and other things that float can travel with the wind a very long way.

■ Balloons rise high

A kite will go up in the sky only when there is wind to carry it. But a balloon filled with gas that is lighter than air will rise even when there is no wind at all.

■ Why do balloons rise?

Some balloons are filled with the air you breathe. If you let go of them, they float to the ground. Other balloons are filled with helium, a gas lighter than air. When you let go of them, they float up into the sky. There are also giant balloons that are filled with hot air. They take people on rides in the sky. They can go very high and very far.

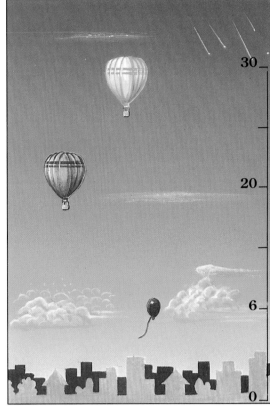

▲ How high balloons can go

■ Why do they stop?

Air high above the ground is thinner than air near the ground. When a balloon gets up this high, the thin air pushes on the balloon with less force. The gas inside the balloon pushes out, increasing the air pressure, making the balloon bigger and bigger until it pops. Other balloons have tiny holes that are too small to see. The gas leaks out, and they fall back to earth.

Pressure

Bang!

Tiny holes

11

❓ How Are Words and Pictures Sent by Telephone Wires?

ANSWER A special machine can send pictures and words. It is called a facsimile, or fax, machine. The machine looks at the dark and light places on a piece of paper and turns them into electrical signals. These signals travel along phone wires. When they reach the end of the line, another fax machine turns them back into pictures and words.

■ A picture goes

The fax machine looks at this picture of a tulip. It divides the picture into strips of very small light and dark points that become electrical signals.

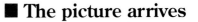

■ The picture arrives

A second fax machine receives the electrical signals. Line by line, it turns them back into light and dark points. It prints them on a piece of paper for you to see.

Phone company

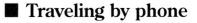

■ Traveling by phone

Fax signals are sent by the phone company the same way as an ordinary telephone call. If the person on the other end lives far away, the signal is made stronger as it goes.

● To the Parent

Fax machines are based on the same principle as black-and-white television. A TV station converts the varying light intensities of a scene, line by line, into electrical signals, which are then broadcast as radio waves from an antenna. A television image is created when an electron beam scans the fluorescent face of the TV screen, laying down each line of the incoming signal in order.

Who Invented Chewing Gum?

ANSWER Gum was first used by Native Americans who lived in Mexico. They made it from the white sap of a local tree. They boiled the sap. Then they let it dry in the sun. The hardened white sap, called chicle, was chewy but did not have any flavor, unlike the gum we chew today.

■ **Boiling sap for gum**

Who Sold the First Gum?

In the United States, Thomas Adams had the idea of covering pieces of chicle with hard candy shells, which flavored the gum. At first Adams sold his gum in little round balls. Later, Adams's Chiclets became small, flat pieces.

A man named John Colgan also made gum better. He added a pleasant smell and changed its shape. Colgan sold gum in thin, flat rectangles called sticks. Today, most gum is sold this way.

John Colgan ▶

◀ Thomas Adams

Where Is Chocolate From?

Chocolate also came from Mexico. The Aztec people made chocolate from the beans of the cacao plant. When Hernán Cortés of Spain invaded Mexico and captured the Aztec capital in 1519, his soldiers were served a refreshing but bitter chocolate drink by the Aztecs.

Cacao plant

● To the Parent

Chewing gum was first made from chicle. It came from the sap of the sapodilla tree, which grows in the Yucatán Peninsula. When chicle was introduced to the United States, it had an unpleasant smell and no taste of its own. Thomas Adams gave it a more pleasant flavor by adding a candy coating. John Colgan added fragrance. When William Wrigley Jr. added sugar and flavoring of cinnamon or mint, chewing gum became popular.

15

Why Do Doughnuts Have Holes?

(ANSWER) Doughnuts are made by mixing flour, sugar, eggs, and other ingredients. The batter is shaped like a ring. Then it is fried in hot oil. People tell different stories about why doughnuts have holes, but one thing is certain. The hole in the middle lets it cook evenly on the inside and outside.

▲ Doughnuts may have come from another kind of pastry that had a walnut in the middle. Over time, the nut was no longer used. Instead of trying something else, a hole was left in the middle.

▲ Thanks to the hole, heat gets to the middle of a doughnut, and it cooks quickly and evenly.

16

In the word "doughnut," the "dough" is for the batter, but where is the "nut?" The first doughnuts may have looked like small nuts.

■ How about other foods?

Swiss cheese and bagels have holes. So do some breakfast cereals. Canned pineapple also has holes. When it is cut up, the hard center of the fruit is removed. Each slice in the can has a hole in the middle.

There is another story people tell about how doughnuts started: Around 1850, an American boy named Gregory Hanson told his mother to put a hole in the middle of her fried round cakes so they would cook more evenly. She was happy to find out that her son was right.

● **To the Parent**

The true story of the invention of this popular pastry is not known. There is evidence dating back to ancient Greece of breads baked in a doughnut shape. A true doughnut is a small sweetened cake fried in oil. Not all doughnuts have holes. Some have sweet fillings instead.

Why Is Macaroni Hollow?

ANSWER Long ago, merchants who traveled in the desert ate meals made mostly from wheat flour. Carrying the flour and cooking it at the end of the day was difficult. So, before they left home, they mixed the flour with water and made it into shapes that they then dried. They discovered that the shapes dried faster if they were hollow. To make them soft again, they just had to soak them in water. That's how macaroni began.

▼ In ancient Rome, before there was macaroni, people ate gruel, a kind of thick soup made from lightly boiled wheat flour.

■ **A desert caravan**

■ Spaghetti from Italy

It is said that spaghetti was first eaten in Naples, Italy. From there it quickly spread through Europe and today is found all around the world.

■ Chinese noodles

In China there were also long, thin noodles that looked like spaghetti. They were made by mixing soybean or rice flour with water.

19

? Why Are Eggs White and Yellow?

(ANSWER) Each part of an egg helps a baby bird grow. The yellow part is called the yolk. There is a tiny, white spot on the yolk where the baby starts growing. Look closely at a raw egg and you can see this spot, called a blastodisk. As the chick gets bigger, it uses the yolk and the egg white for food. The egg white also has another important job. Like a soft cushion, it protects the chick in its shell.

■ Parts of an egg

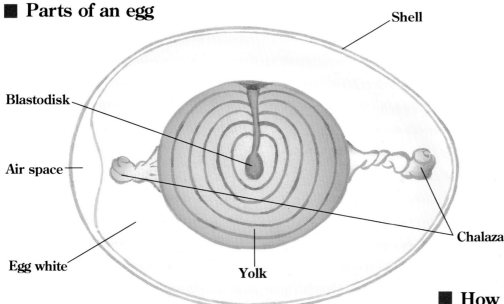

Shell

Blastodisk

Air space

Chalaza

Egg white

Yolk

■ How a chick grows inside the egg

A hen lays an egg. Then she sits on it to keep the egg warm until it hatches. After three days, the heart and blood vessels of the chick have formed. After one week, the eyes can be clearly seen. At two weeks, the growing chick has most of what it needs, including feathers. Three weeks after the egg was laid, the chick breaks out of its shell.

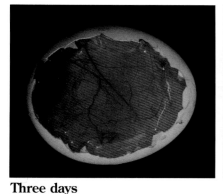

Three days

Two weeks

■ Other animal eggs

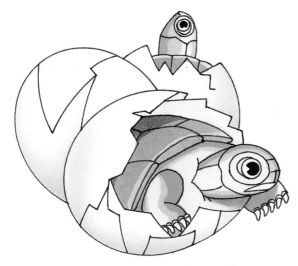

▲ **Turtles.** Like all reptiles, turtles lay eggs on the land. The sun warms the ground, which helps protect the growing baby. A baby turtle has a point on its beak, called an egg tooth. The baby uses it to break out of its shell.

▶ **Frogs.** Most frogs lay their eggs in ponds or streams. Unlike bird eggs, frog eggs have clear, soft shells. When they hatch, tiny tadpoles swim out. The tadpoles live in the water. As they grow, they change into adult frogs.

▼ **Fish.** Fish lay eggs in water. The warmth of the water helps protect the eggs. When baby fish hatch, they are called fry. The egg yolk is still attached to the fry. The young fish use the yolk for food.

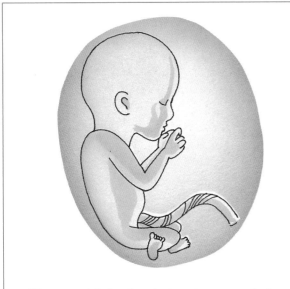

▲ **Humans.** A baby also starts out as an egg but not inside a shell. Human babies grow inside a woman's womb. It takes about nine months for a human baby to develop and be born.

● To the Parent

The blastodisk, the white spot on the surface of the yolk in chicken eggs, becomes the embryo. It grows by taking nourishment from the yolk and the albumen (the white). As a hen is laying an egg, it spins around inside her, causing part of the white to twirl into a cordlike structure called a chalaza. You see this when you look at a raw egg. Chickens begin laying eggs when they are six to seven months old. Hens that are bred as egg layers may produce over 250 per year.

❓ Why Isn't a Football Round?

ANSWER Long before people played football, they played other ball games. They used all sorts of things for balls. In ancient Greece they took the part of a pig called the bladder and filled it with air. The Greeks used the egg-shaped bladder as a ball. Perhaps this is where the football shape comes from.

▲ **Egg-shaped bladder**

■ **A Greek ball game**

■ A sturdier ball wrapped in leather

A pig's bladder filled with air is not very sturdy. Later, people tried covering the bladder with leather. They also stuffed the inside with feathers, leaves, or hair. When the game of rugby was developed in England, it used a ball with this same shape. Rugby is one of the games that led to the development of American football.

■ Some different balls

Many sports use balls. The round shape is ideal for rolling and bouncing. Some balls are filled with air. Others are solid.

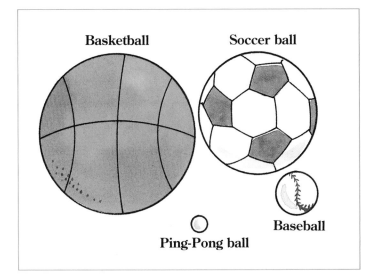

▲ In the United States football developed from the sport of rugby. In rugby the ball can be kicked as in soccer, but it can also be carried or passed as in American football. Players bump into one another more in American football than in rugby. That's why football players wear shoulder pads, helmets, and other equipment designed to protect them.

● To the Parent

About 4,000 years ago the Egyptians played a game using a stone ball. In the second century AD an egg-shaped ball made from the bladder of a pig was used, and in the 12th century a ball was made by wrapping a pig bladder in leather and stuffing it with hair, leaves, or feathers. American football developed from the rough-and-tumble game of rugby. According to one story, rugby began in England during a soccer match. One of the players, a student named William Webb Ellis, suddenly picked up the ball and carried it over the goal line. Although this is against soccer's rules, it led to the development of a sport in which the ball is carried.

❓ Why Aren't the Olympic Games Played Every Year?

ANSWER The Olympics began in ancient times. According to one legend, they were started by the Greek hero named Hercules when he and his three brothers ran a race. To honor their hero, the Greeks decided to hold more contests. Since there were four brothers in all, they held the events once every four years.

■ **Ancient Olympians**

■ The modern Olympics

The ancient Olympics ended when Greece was conquered by Rome. The games were not played again for 1,500 years. The modern Olympics were started by Baron Pierre de Coubertin of France. He saw the games as a way for the people of different countries to get to know each other. The modern Olympics have been played since 1896. In 1924 a separate Olympics was started for winter sports.

■ Now every two years

In the past, the summer and winter Olympics were held in the same year. Beginning in 1994 they started to take place alternately every two years. The pink boxes in this chart show when the summer and winter Olympics will be held.

Summer	1994	1995	1996	1997	1998	1999	2000
Winter	1994	1995	1996	1997	1998	1999	2000

❓ How Did the Atmosphere Form?

ANSWER The air around the earth is called the atmosphere. It was formed a long, long time ago when our planet was very young. Back then there were many volcanoes. The volcanoes erupted, sending out thick clouds of steam and other gases that had been trapped inside the earth. The steam turned into violent storm clouds that rained down on the earth to form the oceans. The gases collected just above the planet. Over millions of years they changed into the air we breathe today.

A bigger moon

When the earth was first formed the moon was much closer, so it looked bigger in the sky.

How air was made

1 Volcanoes erupt, sending gases out of the earth. They form a thick blanket of carbon dioxide, nitrogen, and water vapor around the planet.

2 As the planet cools, thick clouds develop. Many years of rain form the oceans. The carbon dioxide is absorbed back into the seas. The atmosphere is now mainly nitrogen gas.

3 Tiny plants called algae develop in the ocean. They use carbon dioxide and sunlight to make food. They give off oxygen, which begins to collect in the atmosphere.

4 The air has formed. It is rich in nitrogen and oxygen. It also has small amounts of other gases, like carbon dioxide, plus dust and water.

● To the Parent

Earth's atmosphere is about 300 miles thick and has four layers: the troposphere (0-10 miles), where weather develops; the stratosphere (10-30 miles), where ozone absorbs harmful radiation; the mesosphere (30-50 miles), the coldest layer; and the thermosphere, where the air is thinnest.

? Why Is Snow White?

ANSWER Each snowflake is made of frozen water. Like water and ice, snowflakes are really clear. But they look white because of the way light shines on them. The light bounces off snow in all directions. That makes the snow look white to us.

▲ A snowflake is clear

■ Snowflakes and light

In this picture, light shines on a group of snowflakes. It bounces off in all directions.

■ Glass is also clear

When light passes through a single piece of glass, the glass looks clear. But when glass is broken into very tiny pieces, it reflects light in all directions. Then it looks white, like snow.

◀ **Powdered glass**

■ Salt

Salt is also made from tiny, clear crystals. When a great number of these square crystals are together they look white just as snow does.

❓ How Many Languages Are There?

ANSWER There are almost too many languages to count. The world is divided into many countries. People in every country speak at least one language. In some countries people speak many different languages. When you add them up, there are 3,000 to 5,000 languages spoken around the world.

■ Some major languages

Europe

Each country has its own language, but some of the main languages in Europe are English, French, German, Italian, Russian, and Spanish.

In French, people greet each other by saying "Bonjour." In German, they say "Guten Tag." In Russian, it's "Privet."

Common greetings in English are "Hi" or "Hello" and "Good morning."

North America

Many languages are spoken on this continent, but most people speak English, Spanish, or French.

Africa

Some of the major languages in Africa are Swahili, French, English, and Arabic.

In countries where Spanish is spoken, people greet each other by saying "Buenos días."

South America

Most people here speak Spanish or Portuguese, but among the other languages spoken are Dutch and English.

■ Languages in India

India has more languages than any other country. There are more than 800 in this crowded country. Some people say the language changes every 12 miles.

Asia

Some of the main languages spoken here are Chinese, Japanese, English, and Arabic.

When speaking Mandarin Chinese, two people greet by saying "Ni hao."

Oceania

The main languages spoken on the many islands here are English, Fijian, Samoan, and Tongan.

● To the Parent

Some languages are spoken by many millions of people; others are used by a few dozen or perhaps even fewer. The languages used by the largest numbers of people are Mandarin Chinese, English, Hindi, and Spanish. In countries where there are many languages, there is often a common language that many people understand, such as Swahili in Africa and Hindi and English in India. Languages developed in separated regions where there was little interaction between the cultures. Today many languages are spoken within the borders of diversely populated countries like the United States.

? Why Does Your Voice Sound Different on Tape?

ANSWER When you speak, you hear your voice two ways. Sound travels through the air to your ears. It also goes through the bones in your head to your ears. When you play your voice on a tape recorder you hear only the sound that comes through the air. That is why it sounds a bit different.

■ **Record your voice**

■ **Hearing your voice**

Sound travels in waves you cannot see. The air carries these waves and so do the bones in your head. Your brain combines all this information, and you hear your own voice. The arrows in the pictures below show how the sound travels.

▲ **Through your bones**

▲ **Through the air**

When you play a tape recording of your voice, you may be surprised by the way your voice sounds. If someone else is listening, he will not be surprised at all. To him, your voice sounds the way it always does.

■ Listen to your voice

The sound of your voice that comes from the tape does not travel through the bones in your head. Instead you hear your voice as it sounds to other people all the time.

? Did Fish Really Fall from the Sky like Rain?

■ **It's raining fish!**

ANSWER It sounds amazing, but it is true. One famous case happened almost 100 years ago in Europe. It has happened since then in other places. The falling fish were probably caused by a waterspout. That's a tornado that travels over water. The waterspout sucked the fish into the air. Then when the waterspout moved over the land, the fish fell out of the sky like rain.

■ It also rained frogs

It happened about 10 years ago in England. Frogs fell after a heavy rain. There is also a report that it rained crabs in England.

?? What Happens?

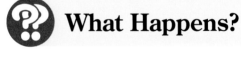

A whirling waterspout travels over a body of water. Like an enormous vacuum cleaner, it sucks up everything in its path. As the water goes up, so do the fish swimming in it. When the waterspout passes over land, the water drops as rain—and the fish fall, too.

● To the Parent

There are records in Europe and the United States of fish falling during a very heavy downpour. There have also been reports of frogs, crabs, coins, and even seeds. In all likelihood these were caused by a waterspout or a tornado drawing objects into the air and then depositing them elsewhere. A waterspout is a tornado that sucks water up from the ocean or a large lake. The spout may be several hundred feet tall and last for half an hour. Waterspouts are common in the tropics but occur in higher latitudes as well.

Did You Know That Ocean Water Contains Gold and Silver?

ANSWER The earth's oceans were formed long ago. Throughout thousands of years, water washing over the land has carried bits of rock and mineral into the water. Some minerals give the ocean its salty taste. Also dissolved in ocean water are large amounts of the valuable minerals gold and silver.

▲ **Gold** is used to make jewelry, coins, and other treasures. The oceans are believed to have almost 15 million tons of dissolved gold.

▲ **Silver,** like gold, is used in many valuable objects. Some experts say the oceans could hold nearly 36 million tons of silver.

▲ **Uranium** plays an important role in producing nuclear energy. The oceans are said to contain over 4 billion tons of this element.

▲ Removing salt from seawater

■ Dissolved in the seas

Chlorine and sodium are the two elements that make salt. They are the most common elements found in seas and oceans. In some parts of the world, people get the salt they need from ocean water. The chart below shows how abundant sodium and chlorine are.

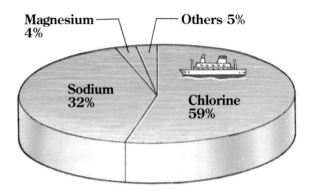

Magnesium 4%

Others 5%

Sodium 32%

Chlorine 59%

❓ What About on Land?

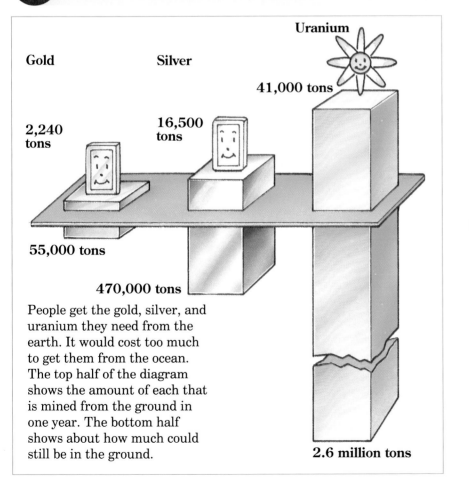

Gold

Silver

Uranium

41,000 tons

2,240 tons

16,500 tons

55,000 tons

470,000 tons

2.6 million tons

People get the gold, silver, and uranium they need from the earth. It would cost too much to get them from the ocean. The top half of the diagram shows the amount of each that is mined from the ground in one year. The bottom half shows about how much could still be in the ground.

● To the Parent

Ocean water is rich in dissolved minerals. By far the most abundant are those that make salt. In some countries salt is still produced in salt fields where seawater is evaporated. There are also valuable minerals dissolved in ocean water, including gold, silver, and uranium. Because of the vastness of the earth's oceans, obtaining these precious metals from the water is extremely difficult. Recent efforts have been made to extract uranium, which is the most plentiful of the three in ocean water. So far the process has proved to be much more expensive than extracting it from the earth.

Why Does Some Glue Work So Fast?

ANSWER All glues feel sticky when you first touch them. But they are not all the same. Most glues take a while to harden and hold things together. A few glues are made to work very quickly. The fast ones are called instant glue.

Instant glue sticks very quickly. It also holds things tightly together. Once two objects are glued together, it is very hard to pull them apart.

■ How instant glue works

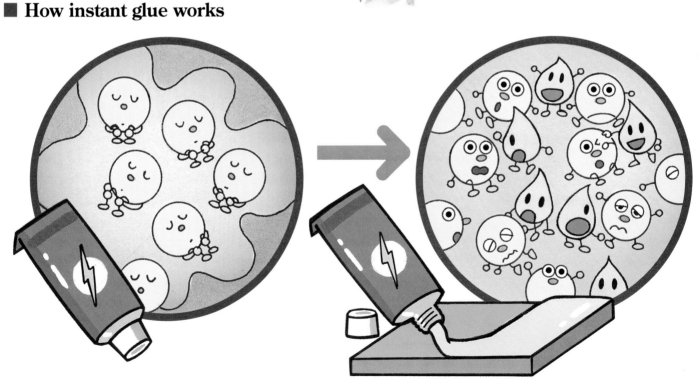

▲ Inside a closed tube, instant glue is not working. The tiny glue particles rest until the tube is opened.

▲ When the glue comes out, the air touches it. Water in the air wakes up the glue, and it starts to harden.

What Else Is Sticky?

■ Sticky situations

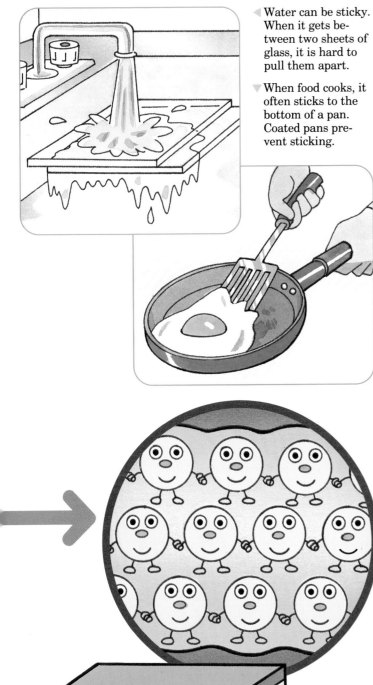

◁ Water can be sticky. When it gets between two sheets of glass, it is hard to pull them apart.

▽ When food cooks, it often sticks to the bottom of a pan. Coated pans prevent sticking.

▲ When the instant glue is spread between two objects, it takes from 10 seconds to 1 minute to harden and hold them together tightly.

Things often stick together without glue. When that happens, something else is taking the place of glue. One good example is water. We think of it as being very slippery, but sometimes it can be sticky.

■ Glue fills the space

Almost all objects have an uneven surface. Glue fits into the space between two surfaces. When the glue dries, it locks the two objects together.

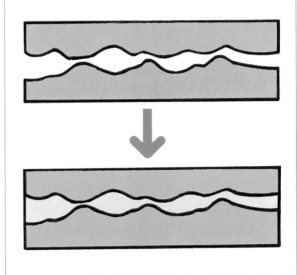

●To the Parent

Instant glue hardens quickly as it absorbs water from the air. Instant glue is lightweight and has great strength, so it is very useful. For example, it is used with rivets in assembling airplane fuselages to help prevent metal fatigue. Instant glue also plays a role as an adhesive in surgery.

? Why Do Some Objects Feel Warm While Others Feel Cool?

ANSWER When you touch the metal chain on a swing, it feels cool to your hand. At the same time, the swing seat of wood or plastic feels warmer. How can this be? When you touch an object, some heat leaves your hand and goes into that object. If something takes away a lot of heat, it feels cool to your hand. If it takes away less heat, it feels warmer.

■ Feel the difference

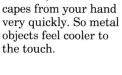

Metal. When you touch something made of metal, the heat escapes from your hand very quickly. So metal objects feel cooler to the touch.

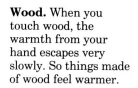

Wood. When you touch wood, the warmth from your hand escapes very slowly. So things made of wood feel warmer.

How Does Touch Work?

Just beneath your skin are nerve endings called receptors. They are connected by nerves to your brain. Different receptors have different jobs. Some sense pressure. Others feel pain. Certain receptors feel hot or cold. They help your brain know when heat is leaving your hand.

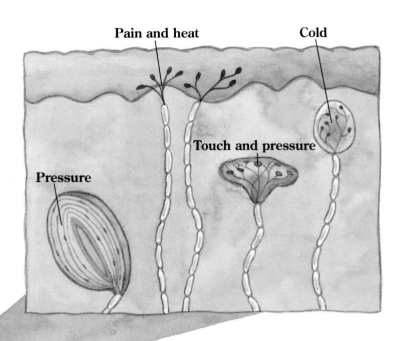

Pain and heat　**Cold**

Touch and pressure

Pressure

■ Many nerve endings

You have nerve endings for hot and cold where they help you the most. For instance, you have lots of them on your tongue, hands, and fingers. You have fewer of them at other places such as your thighs and back. So these places do not sense hot and cold as well.

● To the Parent

Iron is an excellent conductor of heat. That is why it draws heat from your hand, making iron objects feel cool even at room temperature. People sense hot and cold because of specific nerve receptors, located just beneath the surface of the skin. The number of receptors varies throughout the body. The greatest concentrations are on the tip of the tongue, the fingertips, the back of the hand, the instep of the foot, and the chest.

?Did You Know Some Metal Can Remember Its Shape?

ANSWER If you bend a metal paper clip, it stays that way unless you bend it back. When you bend it back, it may not look exactly the same as it did before you bent it. Most metal objects are like that. But a few metals are different. They can change their shape and then go back to the way they were. It's almost as if they remember the way they used to look.

■ How it works

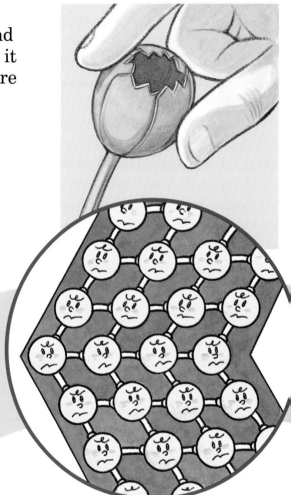

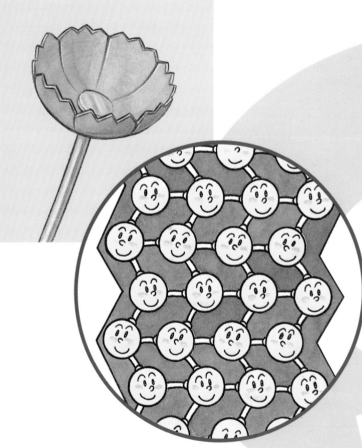

2. Now we squeeze the flower shut to change its shape. This makes the particles change the way they hold onto each other, but they still stay together.

1. Let's start with some special metal that has been shaped like an open flower. It is made of tiny particles that are too small to see. This drawing shows how the particles of metal are lined up.

4. Now the particles have returned to the way they were lined up when the flower was first made. The flower is open once again.

■ Remembering its shape

At most temperatures you can fold or bend this special metal, and it stays that way. At very hot temperatures the metal acts differently. It "remembers" the way it used to look. The particles line up as before to form its original shape.

▲ Someday a large antenna in space may be made of this special metal. The antenna would be folded into a small package and carried into space by a spaceship. Once in orbit, it would be released. The sun's heat would cause the antenna to open, just like the metal flower we placed in hot water.

3. Next we place the closed flower in hot water. The heat makes the metal particles start changing back to the way they were.

●To the Parent

Metal that remembers its original shape is called a shape-memory alloy. Even if it is bent or folded, it returns to its first shape when heated. Many shape-memory alloys have been developed for industrial and medical use. They could also be used in space. For instance, a huge parabolic antenna could be folded up into a tiny package for easy transport into space. Once there, the sun's heat would return the antenna to its original shape.

Why Are Some People Left-Handed?

(ANSWER) Most people use their right hand to draw a picture or throw a ball. Some people, however, do these things better with their left hand. It all depends on your brain. The human brain has two halves. In right-handed people the left side has more control. In left-handed people it works the other way. The right side of the brain is stronger.

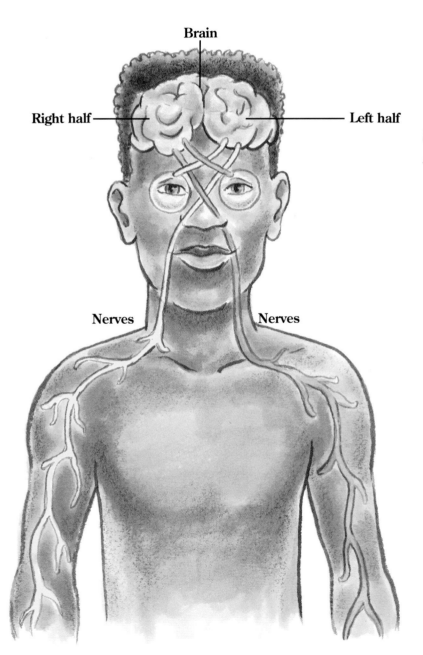

Brain

Right half — **Left half**

Nerves **Nerves**

Sometimes being left-handed has its advantages. Playing baseball is one example. Many more people are right-handed than left-handed, so most pitchers are right-handed. A left-handed batter often is able to hit better against those pitchers.

Right and left sides

The brain has two halves. The nerves connected to them control the way your body moves. In the drawing, you can see how the nerves cross over. Some nerves go from the left half of the brain to the right side of the body. Others go from the right half of the brain to the left side. That is why the left half of your brain controls the right side of your body and the right half controls the left side.

Since most people are right-handed, most tools and equipment are made to be held in the right hand. This includes many common objects such as scissors, can openers, and guitars. Left-handed people must learn to use these right-handed items or find ones made especially for them.

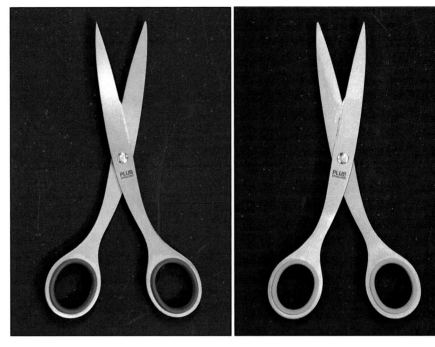

▲ Right-handed scissors   ▲ Left-handed scissors

?? What About Feet?

Right-handed people also favor their right foot and are stronger in the right leg. When they go left around a track, their right leg is on the outside. This makes running around the curves easier. Most people are right-handed, so track races are run to the left.

● To the Parent

The brain's cerebrum controls the sensory functions and movement of the body. It is divided into left and right hemispheres, which perform almost the same operations. Normally one hemisphere or the other is dominant. In newborn babies the orientation may not be obvious. Usually by the time the child is one year old, the dominant side can be recognized. When it is the left half of the brain, one becomes right-handed, and when it is the right half, one becomes left-handed. Many more people are right-handed. Only about 5 percent of men and 3 percent of women are left-handed.

❓ Do the Same Fish Live in Fresh Water and Salt Water?

ANSWER Some fish live in the ocean where it is salty. If you put them in fresh water they would die. Other fish live in lakes, rivers, and ponds where the water is fresh instead of salty. They would die in the ocean. Only a few fish can live in both fresh water and salt water.

■ From river to ocean

A freshwater fish cannot live in salt water because salt removes water from the fish's body. The fish dries up and dies.

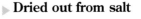

▶ **Dried out from salt**

■ From ocean to river

An ocean fish needs salt water to live. In fresh water, its body cannot get rid of liquid. The fish gets swollen, and then it dies.

▲ Swollen with water

 # Which Live in Both?

Some fish can adjust to both salty and fresh water. Salmon are born in fresh water. The young salmon swim down rivers into the ocean, where they live as adults. Later, they swim back up the rivers to lay their eggs in fresh water. Some eels live in both kinds of water, too.

▲ Salmon swim upstream.

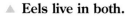

▲ Eels live in both.

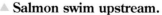

● To the Parent

The internal organs of saltwater fish are specially designed to eliminate salt while taking in adequate water. Freshwater fish are not able to eliminate the excess salt, so when placed in salt water take in more salt than their bodies can handle. Most fish can live in only one environment. Some salmon, however, live in the ocean and spawn in rivers. To get used to the change of water, they stay near the mouth of the river for a while before going upstream. Some eels are born in the ocean but go into rivers to mature. They return to the ocean to spawn.

Why Do Ocean Fish Come in So Many Different Shapes?

(ANSWER) The oceans are huge. There are many different kinds of places in them. There is deep water and shallow water. There are cold open seas and warm coral reefs. Fish live in all these places. A fish's shape, size, and color fit the place where it lives.

■ Fish in coral reefs

Many fish in the reef have narrow bodies. Their thin shape makes it easier for them to swim in and out of the coral. The fish often have stripes on the sides of their bodies that blend in with the branches of coral. That makes it harder for other fish to see and catch them.

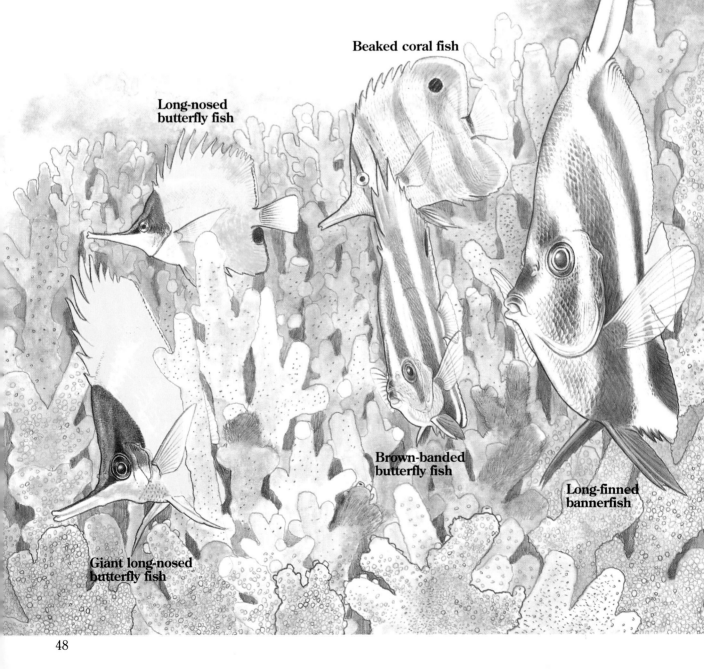

Beaked coral fish

Long-nosed butterfly fish

Brown-banded butterfly fish

Long-finned bannerfish

Giant long-nosed butterfly fish

■ Some ocean fish are fast swimmers

Tuna live in the open sea. Their sleek, pointed bodies help them move through the water very fast. That helps them catch the smaller fish they eat and escape from bigger fish that want to eat them.

■ Bottom dwellers

Certain fish such as flounder lie on the ocean floor. Their color and pattern make their flat bodies very hard to see because they blend into the sandy bottom. It is difficult for their enemies to find them.

● To the Parent

Fish have evolved to adapt to the places where they live. In addition to the examples above, there are flying fish, whose pectoral fins function like wings. When attacked by larger fish, flying fish glide above the surface of the ocean to escape. Sea horses wrap their tails around floating seaweed. This tactic helps to camouflage them and protect them from predators, who think they are part of the seaweed.

Why Don't Baby Whales Drown When They Are Born?

(ANSWER) Whales are not fish. They need to breathe air just as people do. A baby whale is born underwater. Its mother pushes it to the surface to take its first breath. Baby whales are good swimmers right from the start. When they need air, they swim to the surface and breathe. When they go back under, they hold their breath.

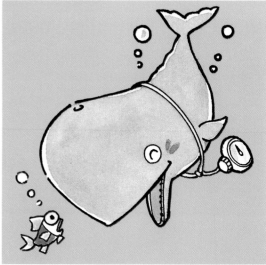

▲ **Holding its breath**

■ The birth of a whale

A whale calf is born in the ocean. It can swim all by itself as soon as it is born.

How Big Is a Baby Whale?

The blue whale is the largest animal that ever lived. It can be as long as 100 feet. Even a baby blue whale is huge. It is 23 to 30 feet long and weighs about 3 tons. One newborn blue whale calf weighs about as much as 1,000 human babies.

1 baby whale   1,000 human babies

23 to 30 feet

A whale breathes air

●To the Parent

A mother whale guides her newborn calf to the surface to take its first breath. Like all mammals, a baby whale is raised on mother's milk. A nursing whale's breasts are concealed inside her body so they won't slow her down while swimming. She lets them out only when the baby wants to feed. Whale calves must surface fairly often to breathe. A nursing mother's milk comes out with such force that the time spent drinking underwater is shortened. A baby whale may nurse about 40 times a day. In those feedings it will consume more than 100 gallons of mother's milk.

? How Do Baby Turtles Find the Sea?

ANSWER Baby sea turtles are born on land at night. As soon as they hatch from their shells, the babies crawl quickly toward the sea. To find the water, they go downhill toward the light of the moon shining on the ocean.

The mother sea turtle climbs up on land. She digs a hole on the beach and lays her eggs in it. Then she returns to the sea.

When the babies hatch they are very small and cannot protect themselves from large animals who might want to eat them. They must quickly get to the safety of the sea.

■ **Crawling to the sea**

It's called instinct

Baby turtles do not have to learn where the sea is. Somehow they know how to find it. This is called instinct. The babies naturally crawl downhill, and they are attracted to the light of the moon on the water. These clues help them find their way.

How Do Turtle Eggs Make Girls and Boys?

When a sea turtle egg is laid, it is not certain if a boy or girl turtle will grow inside. It depends on the temperature. If the egg is in a place where the sun warms it, the baby will be a female. If the egg is in a cool place, it will produce a male.

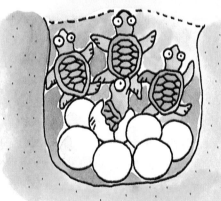

▲ Cool eggs make boys.

▲ Warm eggs make girls.

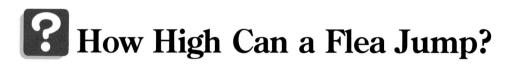

How High Can a Flea Jump?

(ANSWER) A flea can jump up almost 8 inches. That is amazing for such a tiny insect, generally about ⅛-inch long. A flea jumps 70 times its own height. If it were as tall as a person, a flea could leap over a tall building.

■ **A powerful jump**

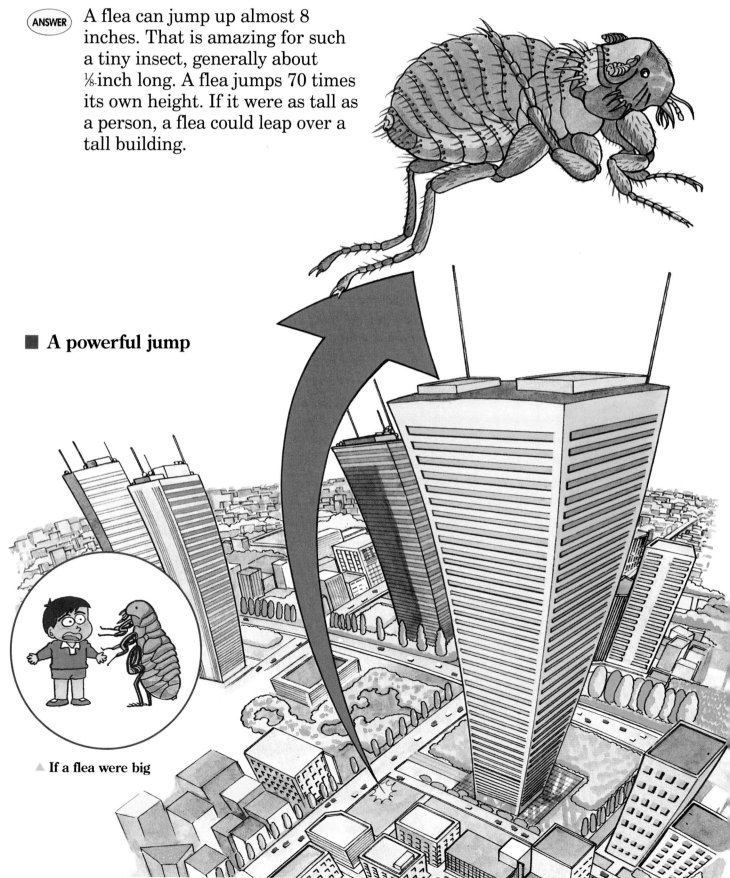

▲ **If a flea were big**

■ How many times their height?

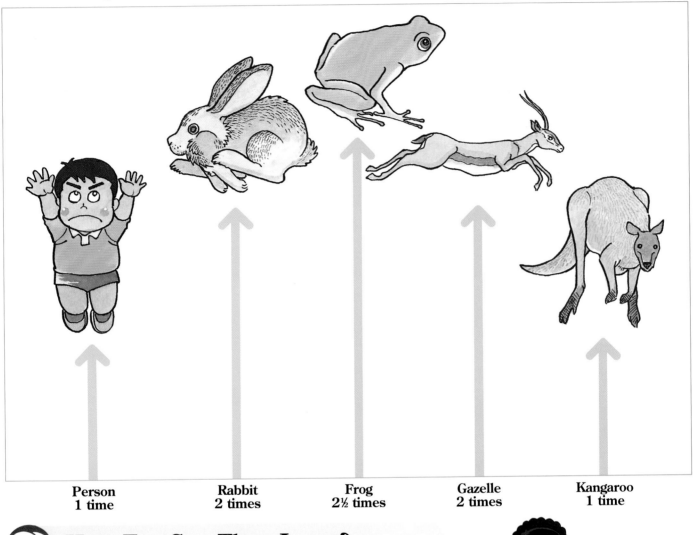

Person	Rabbit	Frog	Gazelle	Kangaroo
1 time	2 times	2½ times	2 times	1 time

How Far Can They Jump?

A flea can also jump very far for its size. When a flea leaps, it often lands more than a foot away. That's about 100 times its height. The chart below shows how far some other animals can jump. Each number is how many times its height the animal jumps.

	Person 4½ times		**Frog** 15 times
	Flea 100 times		**Gazelle** 8 times
	Rabbit 2 times		**Kangaroo** 7 times

❓ Why Do Elephants Have Big Ears?

(ANSWER) Elephants are large animals. In places where the weather is hot, they get very warm. An elephant's big ears help it to stay cool. They get rid of extra heat that the animal does not need.

■ Home on the plains

In Africa, elephants live on hot plains called savannas. There are few trees to protect them from the sun. That's why those large ears are so important.

■ Ears as coolers

An elephant's ears have many blood vessels. They bring warm blood to the surface where the heat goes into the air. That makes the elephant feel cooler.

▲ African elephant　　▲ Indian elephant　　▲ Mammoth

Elephants live in the wild in Africa and Asia. African elephants need large ears to get rid of heat on the savanna. Asian elephants live in areas with forests. Since they can cool off in the shade, they have developed smaller ears. The mammoth is an ancestor of today's elephants. It lived long ago in cold weather. The mammoth needed to keep its body heat to stay warm, so it had small ears and was covered with fur.

● To the Parent

Like all warm-blooded animals, the elephant has developed a mechanism to get rid of unwanted heat. It flaps its large ears, releasing warmth from its body into the air. Since African elephants evolved in hotter, sunnier habitats, their ears are larger than those of Asian elephants. Other warm-blooded animals regulate heat different ways. Dogs pant allowing heat to escape from their tongues. When humans sweat, they release excess heat.

? How Long Do Animals Live?

(ANSWER) There are many different kinds of animals in the world. How long they live depends on the kind of animal. Some live for less than a day. Others keep going for 100 years or even longer. Most people live for about 70 years.

■ How long animals live

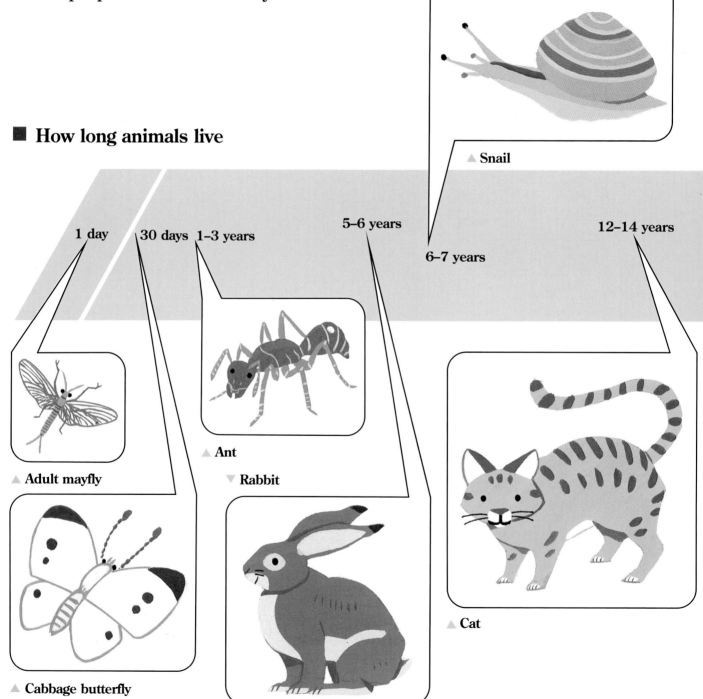

▲ Snail

1 day | 30 days | 1–3 years

5–6 years

6–7 years

12–14 years

▲ Adult mayfly

▲ Ant   ▼ Rabbit

▲ Cabbage butterfly

▲ Cat

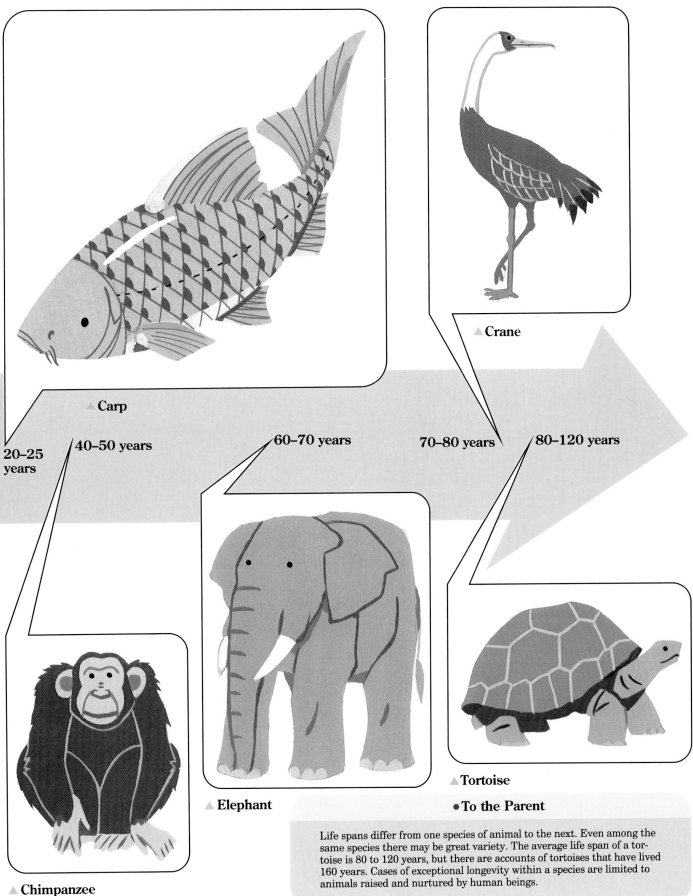

▲ Carp

▲ Crane

20–25 years

40–50 years

60–70 years

70–80 years

80–120 years

▲ Chimpanzee

▲ Elephant

▲ Tortoise

● To the Parent

Life spans differ from one species of animal to the next. Even among the same species there may be great variety. The average life span of a tortoise is 80 to 120 years, but there are accounts of tortoises that have lived 160 years. Cases of exceptional longevity within a species are limited to animals raised and nurtured by human beings.

? What Is the Biggest Animal?

The blue whale, a mammal, is the largest animal of all. It is 100 feet long. The whale shark is the biggest fish in the ocean. It grows to a length of about 42 feet. The giant redfish of the Amazon River is the largest freshwater fish. It grows to a length of more than 8 feet. And the African elephant is 10 feet high at its shoulders, making it the biggest animal on land.

▲ African elephant

■ **Some of the biggest**

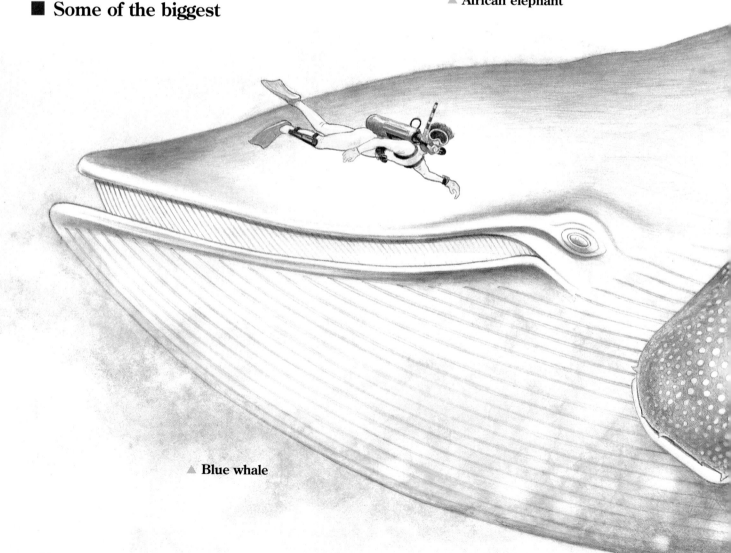

▲ **Blue whale**

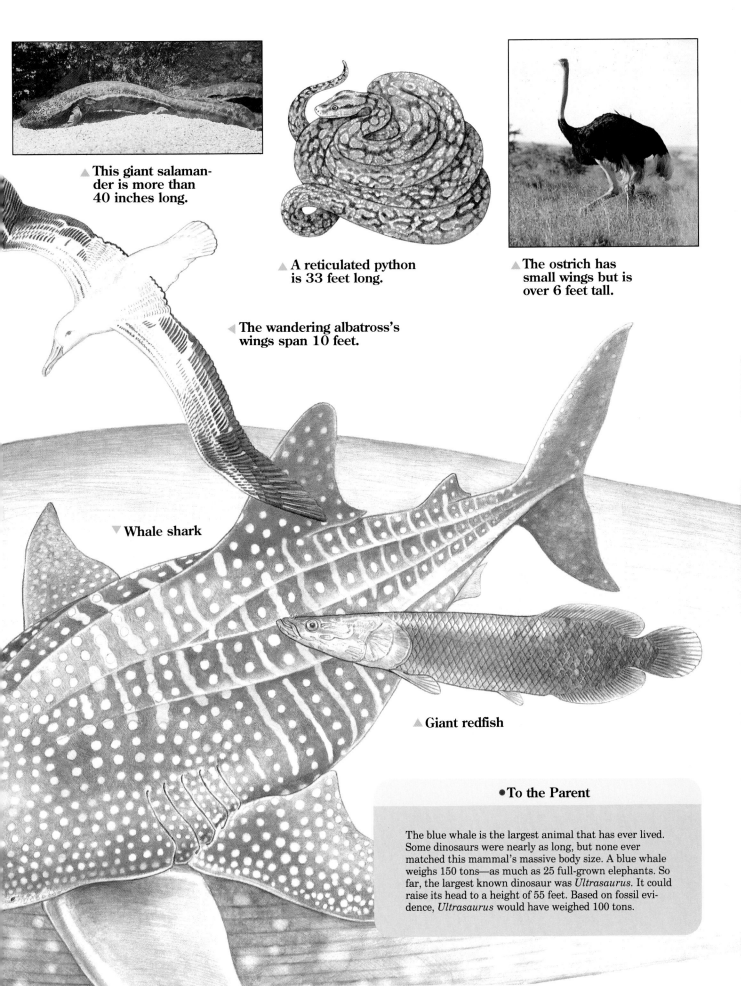

▲ This giant salaman-
der is more than
40 inches long.

▲ A reticulated python
is 33 feet long.

▲ The ostrich has
small wings but is
over 6 feet tall.

◄ The wandering albatross's
wings span 10 feet.

▼ Whale shark

▲ Giant redfish

●To the Parent

The blue whale is the largest animal that has ever lived.
Some dinosaurs were nearly as long, but none ever
matched this mammal's massive body size. A blue whale
weighs 150 tons—as much as 25 full-grown elephants. So
far, the largest known dinosaur was *Ultrasaurus*. It could
raise its head to a height of 55 feet. Based on fossil evidence, *Ultrasaurus* would have weighed 100 tons.

How Small Can Animals Be?

ANSWER One of the tiniest mammals is the pygmy shrew. These furry little creatures live in many places. The one in this picture is from South America. From the tip of its nose to the end of its tail, this mammal is only 3½ inches long. It weighs about as much as a cube of sugar.

■ **A tiny mammal**

■ Small frog

This dink frog lives in Costa Rica and has a body that is about half an inch long. It could sit on a penny with room to spare!

■ Thinnest snake

This nonpoisonous blind snake from the Philippines is very tiny. The one shown here is only about 4 inches long. The snake does have eyes, but they are hidden under the scales on its head, so it can't see well at all.

■ Littlest birds

Hummingbirds are the world's smallest birds. The tiniest one is the male bee hummingbird shown here. It is about 2 inches long and weighs less than a penny. Its nest is a little bit bigger than a quarter. Hummingbirds also lay the smallest eggs of any bird, about ½ inch in diameter.

Which Animals Have Survived since the Dinosaurs?

(ANSWER) The dinosaurs died out 65 million years ago. No animals from their time are still alive today. But there are some creatures that look just like their relatives that lived long ago. In millions and millions of years, these kinds of animals have hardly changed at all.

Horseshoe crabs lived 300 million years ago.

■ Ancient living animals

The coelacanth is an unusual fish. It has two pairs of stumpy fins that look a little like arms and legs. This kind of fish lived about 350 million years ago. It is still found in the waters near Africa.

▶ Coelacanth

Damselflies lived 150 million years ago.

▲ The nautilus lived 500 million years ago.

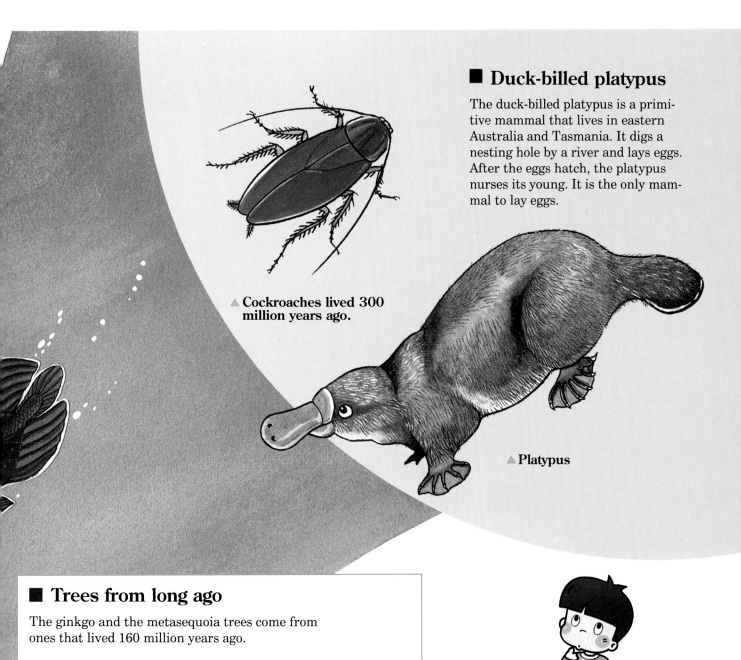

■ Duck-billed platypus

The duck-billed platypus is a primitive mammal that lives in eastern Australia and Tasmania. It digs a nesting hole by a river and lays eggs. After the eggs hatch, the platypus nurses its young. It is the only mammal to lay eggs.

▲ Cockroaches lived 300 million years ago.

▲ Platypus

■ Trees from long ago

The ginkgo and the metasequoia trees come from ones that lived 160 million years ago.

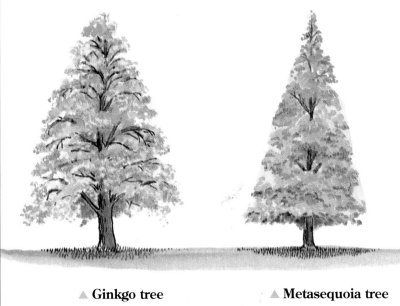

▲ Ginkgo tree   ▲ Metasequoia tree

●To the Parent

The coelacanth belongs to a group of lunged, fleshy-finned prehistoric fish commonly called lobefins. These odd-looking fish, which gave rise to amphibians, were thought to be extinct. Then in 1938 a living coelacanth was found in the deep waters off southern Africa. Since that discovery, other coelacanths have been caught near Madagascar. Other so-called living fossils are remarkably similar to animals that lived hundreds of millions of years ago. They have survived many changes on the planet.

？ Are Bats a Kind of Bird?

(ANSWER) Bats look like birds because they have wings and fly. But they are not birds. They are mammals. Even though they fly, they are very different from birds. Bats do not have feathers, and they don't lay eggs.

■ Bats fly at night

Most birds fly during the day. Bats hang upside down and rest all day. They come out and fly at night.

■ Different animals

Unlike a bird, a bat is covered with fur. Bats also have teeth instead of a beak.

■ Different wings

At the end of a bat's wing are bones that are a bit like the fingers on a person's hand. The wing is made of a thin skin called a membrane. It stretches from one finger to the next. The bones on a bird's wing look very different. A thin skin covers a bird's wing also, but growing out of the skin are feathers.

Look! A bat has five fingers like me.

■ Bats are born live

Bats do not lay eggs as birds do. Bats give birth to live babies like people do. And like all mammals, bats nurse their young. People are mammals, too.

●**To the Parent**

Bats are the only mammals with true flying ability. Unlike other mammals that glide through the air, a bat keeps itself aloft using the muscular movements of its wings. A bat's wing consists of a membrane of skin stretched between the elongated bones of its fingers. Although bats live in nearly every part of the world, they are most common in tropical regions. Like most mammals, bats give birth to live young. Most species bear one or two young in a litter. They typically have one litter a year.

Why Are Some Male Birds More Colorful than Females?

(ANSWER) Sometimes two birds of the same kind look very different. The male bird is covered with colorful feathers. The female bird has dull feathers. The male's bright feathers help him attract a mate. The female's dull feathers help her stay hidden when she sits on her nest.

The female pheasant has dull brown feathers. Their color and pattern blend with the grass. The pheasant's enemies cannot see her sitting on her eggs.

■ **Different roles for males and females**

The male pheasant has bright feathers and colorful markings on his face. When looking for a mate, the male uses his beautiful colors to attract females.

■ Other birds

A male ostrich is covered with shiny black feathers. He has long white plumes on his wings and tail. A female ostrich has dull feathers of gray and brown.

The male and female whydah, or widow bird, also look different. In the mating season it is easy to tell them apart. The male's tail feathers grow very long.

Most of the time the male and female mandarin duck look almost alike. During the mating season, however, the male's feathers turn brilliant colors.

● To the Parent

In many species of birds, males use brightly colored feathers to attract mates. Depending on the type of bird, a courtship display may also include posturing, ritualized movements, or vocalizations. The combination of plumage and display is unique to a species. In many species a nesting female's duller colors camouflage her from predators. Different coloring patterns are not unique to birds. In some fish, males are more brilliantly colored than females.

? Is There Water in a Watermelon?

ANSWER Watermelon is the perfect name for this juicy fruit because it is made up mostly of water. Watermelon vines need lots of sun and water to grow. The fruit has a special way of holding onto water as the plant grows.

■ Inside a watermelon

The fruit of a watermelon is made of many cells. Each tiny cell holds a lot of water. They are called bubble cells.

Water in Other Fruits

Many fruits and vegetables hold a lot of water. The drawings here show some that people like to eat. In each picture the blue part shows how much of the fruit or vegetable is water.

▲ Tomatoes, strawberries, and watermelons are about 90 percent water.

▲ Lemons, muskmelons, grapes, pineapples, and apples are about 80 percent water.

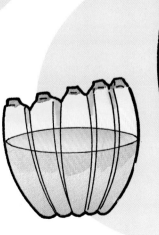

▲ Sweet corn and bananas are about 70 percent water.

![?] What Is the World's Largest Tree?

(ANSWER) The sequoia is the largest tree. Sequoias are biggest because they have the thickest trunks. Some are more than 300 feet high. But there are trees that are even taller. Some redwoods are almost 400 feet tall. The biggest sequoias and redwoods are very old trees. It takes a long time to grow that big.

■ The giant sequoia

Some sequoia trunks measure more than 30 feet across. Long ago a tunnel was cut in the tree that is pictured below. The tunnel is large enough to drive a car through.

■ The biggest flower

The rafflesia plant of Southeast Asia grows the world's largest flower. A single flower can measure 40 inches across and weigh up to 15 pounds. The rafflesia is also one of the worst-smelling flowers in the world. It is sometimes called the stinking corpse lily.

■ The biggest leaves

The water platter is a lotus plant whose leaves float in ponds and lakes in Southeast Asia. Similar plants grow as far away as South America. A single leaf can grow as large as 7 feet across.

MINI-DATA

The 3,500-year-old General Sherman tree in California's Sequoia National Park is the largest living thing on earth. The tree measures 272 feet tall and 36 feet wide.

●**To the Parent**

The largest sequoias are as tall as a 25-story building. A picture of these massive trees is on the cover of this book. The General Sherman tree is the largest tree because of its sheer bulk. It contains enough lumber to build 80 five-room houses. But it is not the tallest tree. This claim goes to a redwood that stands over 394 feet high in Redwood National Park.

73

Why Do Flowers Have So Many Different Shapes?

ANSWER A flower's shape helps it attract insects, like bees and butterflies. Many flowers need insects to spread pollen and make seeds. A flower's shape makes it easier for some insects to visit.

■ **Butterflies drink nectar**

■ Some birds help

Tiny hummingbirds sip the nectar of certain flowers. The shape of these flowers makes it easy for the birds to drink. Then the bird spreads pollen so the flower can make seeds.

Some Flower Shapes

◀ Orchid

◀ Dandelion

▲ Lily

◀ Orchid

◀ Cluster amaryllis

The flower of the cedar tree has no petals to attract animals. Its shape makes it easy for the wind to spread the cedar's pollen.

? How Does Water Climb to the Top of a Tree?

(ANSWER) A tree drinks water through its roots. As the roots take in more and more water, it pushes up through the trunk to the leaves. In some trees the water climbs more than 300 feet.

■ A very large drink

Trees drink a lot of water. For example, take the zelkova tree. This kind of tree grows in Asia but is a relative of the elm tree that grows in the United States. The amount of water it absorbs depends on its size. An average-sized zelkova tree takes in about 2.3 gallons of water a day. That is enough water to fill 44 glasses.

A large oak tree can absorb enough water in one day to fill seven bathtubs.

Carbon dioxide

Oxygen

In addition to water, a tree needs sunlight and air, plus nutrients from the ground. A tree's leaves absorb about 42 quarts of carbon dioxide from the air around it each day. The leaves release about the same amount of oxygen.

A tree uses sunlight, water, and carbon dioxide to make food. Its green leaves produce sugar and starch.

●**To the Parent**

Several forces work together to move water from the roots of a tree up through the trunk and branches to the leaves. As the water in the leaves evaporates, the top of the tree gets drier. As the roots become saturated, water pushes up to the drier areas above. Water molecules stick to one another and to the sides of the tubes through which they move. This phenomenon, called cohesion, helps water go up trees.

Why Does a Tulip Close at Night and Open in the Morning?

(ANSWER) A tulip's petals are open all day. At night the flower feels the colder air and closes its petals. When the warm morning sunlight arrives, the tulip opens again. The changing temperature from day to night makes the flower open and close.

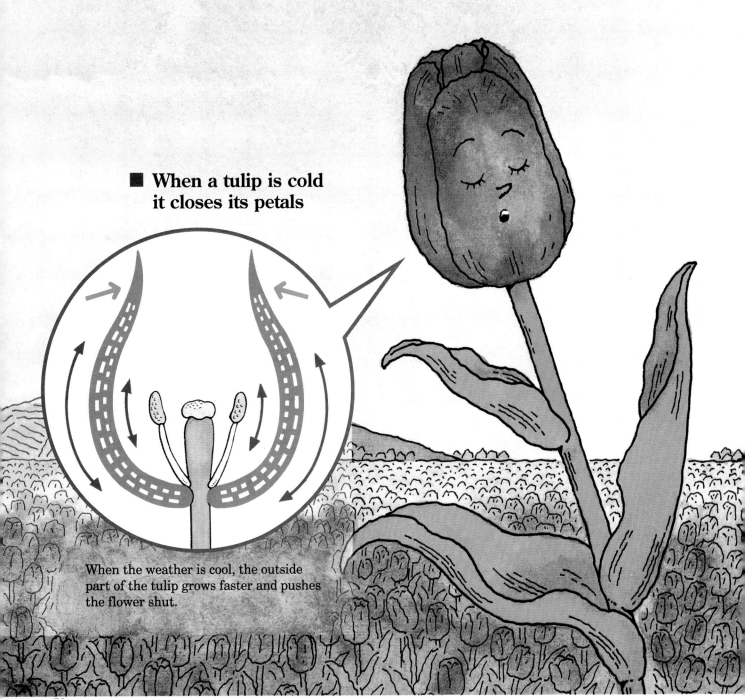

■ **When a tulip is cold it closes its petals**

When the weather is cool, the outside part of the tulip grows faster and pushes the flower shut.

■ Many flowers open

Changing temperatures make tulips open and close. Other flowers do the same thing for a different reason. Gentians and anemones sense changes in the light. When the sun comes up, the flowers open. When it goes down, they close.

▲ Anemone   ▲ Gentian

■ When a tulip is warm it opens its petals

When warm, the inside of the tulip grows faster and pushes the flower open.

? What Are These?

ANSWER These are tern eggs. Their color makes them hard to see among the rocks. Animals who might eat the eggs can't find them.

▲ A leaf fish looks like a fallen leaf floating in the water. Other fish are fooled and don't bother it.

▲ A leafy sea dragon is a relative of the sea horse. It looks like a piece of seaweed floating in the ocean.

▲ A leaf insect has the shape and color of a leaf. When it rests on a plant, the insect seems to disappear.

● To the Parent

Many animals rely on camouflage to protect themselves. An animal's color and shape allow it to blend into its environment and hide from its enemies. The use of camouflage is an effective survival strategy for both predator and prey.

Growing-Up Album

What Country's Greeting Is This?

Here are some people from different countries. Match each person to a greeting in his or her language. The greetings are written across the bottom of the page. A greeting may be used by more than one person.

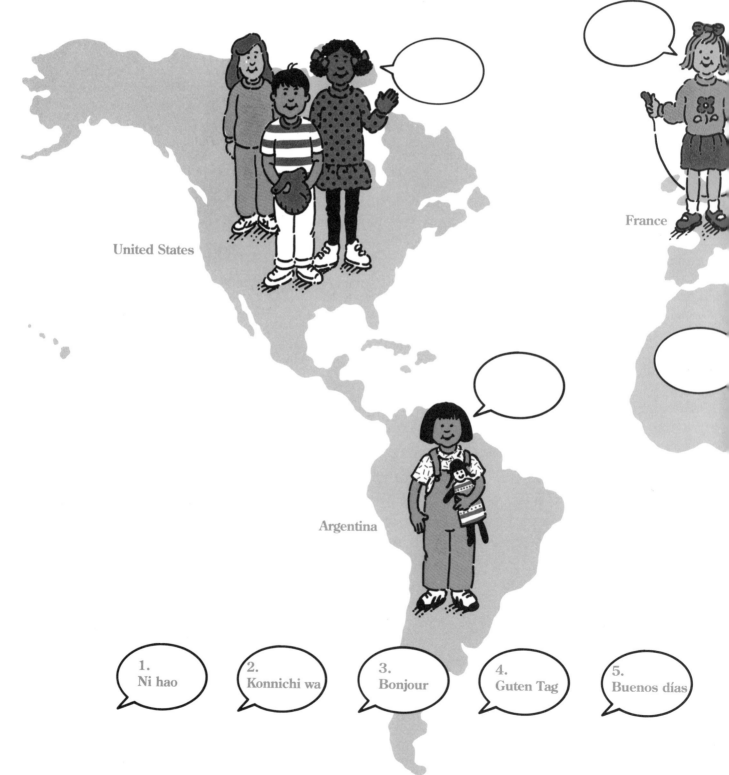

United States

France

Argentina

1. Ni hao

2. Konnichi wa

3. Bonjour

4. Guten Tag

5. Buenos días

Who Lives Longest?

Using the numbers 1 to 5, put these animals in order from the one with the longest life span to the one with the shortest life span. Put the numbers in the boxes.

Crane

Elephant

Tortoise

Carp

Cabbage butterfly

Answers: 1. Tortoise, 2. Crane, 3. Elephant, 4. Carp, 5. Cabbage butterfly.

84

Who Jumps Farthest?

Put a number 1 next to the animal that jumps the farthest compared with the size of its body. Put numbers 2 to 5 in other boxes going from the longest jumpers to the shortest jumpers.

Human ☐

Flea ☐

Frog ☐

Kangaroo ☐

Rabbit ☐

Answers: 1. Flea, 2. Frog, 3. Kangaroo, 4. Human, 5. Rabbit.

Who Has Survived the Ages?

Among the animals below are some whose bodies have hardly changed since the time of the dinosaurs. Put a mark in the box next to these descendants of prehistoric creatures.

Tuna

Nautilus

Octopus

Squid

Whale

Coelacanth

Humans

Horseshoe crab

Answers: Coelacanth, Horseshoe crab, Nautilus.

A Child's First Library of Learning

Staff for
AMAZING FACTS

Managing Editor: Patricia Daniels
Editorial Director: Jean Burke Crawford
Research: Jocelyn Lindsey, Marike van der Veen
Production Manager: Marlene Zack
Copyeditors: Barbara F. Quarmby (Senior), Heidi A. Fritschel
Picture Coordinator: David A. Herod
Production: Celia Beattie
Supervisor of Quality Control: James King
Assistant Supervisor of Quality Control: Miriam Newton
Library: Louise D. Forstall
Computer Composition: Deborah G. Tait (Manager),
    Monika D. Thayer, Janet Barnes Syring, Lillian Daniels

Design/Illustration: Antonio Alcalá, John Jackson,
    David Neal Wiseman
Photography/Illustration: Cover and 73 *(bottom left)*: © Whit
    Bronaugh; 1 and 63 *(center right)*: © Robert A. Tyrrell, El
    Monte, Ca.; 16 *(top right)*, 17 *(top and lower left)*, 35 *(lower
    left)*, 40 and 41 *(top)*: art by Linda Greigg; 20 *(lower left)*
    Photri, Inc.; 23 *(center right)*, 25 *(top right)*, 38 *(top right)*, 44:
    art by Melvin Conrad; 26-27: art by Don Davis; 63 *(lower left
    and top left)*: © Doug Wechsler; 82-83 and 87 *(kids in subma-
    rine)*: art by Gloria Marconi.
Overread: Barbara Klein

Library of Congress Cataloging-in-Publication Data
Amazing Facts.
    p.   cm. – (A Child's First Library of Learning)
    Summary: Answers such questions as "Why are there 7 days
    in a week?" and "Who invented chewing gum?"
    ISBN 0-8094-9459-0 (lib. bdg.).—ISBN 0-8094-9458-2 (trade)
    1. Curiosities and wonders—Juvenile literature.
    2. Handbooks, vade-mecums, etc.—Juvenile literature.
    [1. Curiosities and wonders—Miscellanea. 2. Questions and
    answers.]
    I. Time-Life Books. II. Series.
AG243.A425 1994
031.02–dc20   93-11599
                                              CIP
                                              AC

TIME-LIFE for CHILDREN ®

Managing Editor: Patricia Daniels
Editorial Directors: Jean Burke Crawford, Allan Fallow,
    Karin Kinney, Sara Mark
Director of Marketing: Margaret Mooney
Editorial Coordinator: Marike van der Veen
Editorial Assistant: Mary Saxton

Original English translation by International Editorial Services
Inc./C. E. Berry

First printing. Printed in U.S.A.
Published simultaneously in Canada.

Time Life Inc. is a wholly owned subsidiary of
THE TIME INC. BOOK COMPANY.

TIME LIFE is a trademark of Time Warner Inc. U.S.A.

School and library distribution by Time-Life Education,
P.O. Box 85026, Richmond, Virginia 23285-5026.
For subscription information, call 1-800-621-7026.

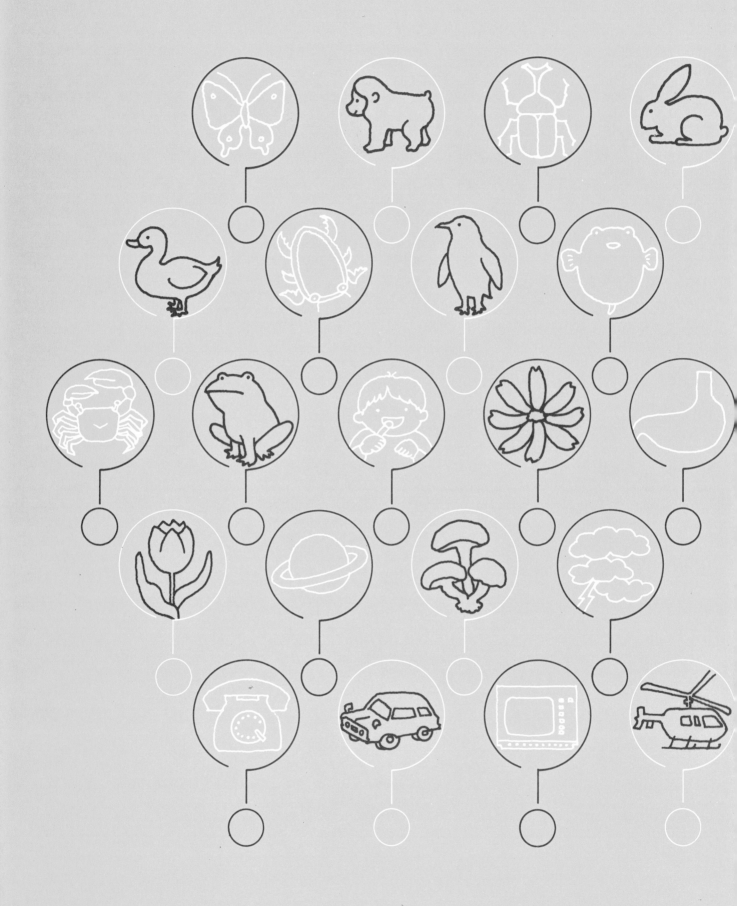